PERE ANTOINE
Marie's teacher
& lifelong friend

Basic black cassock worn by the priest for his daily duties. He carries his rosary.

Black cloak worn over the basic cassock for certain ceremonies and inclement weather. He carries his bible.

MARIE LAVEAU
Age 9

A high waisted sea green school dress of soft cotton mull with pleated flounces at sleeves and neckline and darker ribbon banding at the hem.

An everyday dress of tan cotton with short sleeves, gathered at the waistband. She wears a soft wool, red-fringed shawl and is barefooted.

White silk dress for Sunday Mass with raised decorative stitching at the hemline, 3/4 length elbow puffed sleeves, blue sash, and a scalloped sheer head scarf.

or "Voodoo John"), and he generally conducted these ceremonies. A Voodoo priest is known as a "hungan" or "papa-loa," a priestess is called a "mambo" or "maman-loa." Dr. John was key in creating New Orleans Voodoo, being the first to mix Catholicism and Voodoo snake worship, the first to sell cures as well as hexes, and the first to buy information from servants and slaves about their masters. It was at a St. John's Eve ritual, shortly after the disappearance of her husband Jacques, that Dr. John and the young Marie met. He was impressed by her and began to mentor her as a Voodoo priestess, teaching her many of his spells and other secrets that she would need as a mambo. They worked together until she "married" her second husband, Christophe Glapion.

Marie had developed into a tall, beautiful woman with curly black hair, dusky skin with a reddish tint, and flashing black eyes. She generally wore golden hoops that her father had given her in her ears and she loved dancing and having fun. After she married Glapion she had quit her hairdressing business, devoting her time to the practice of voodoo. She maintained contact with her "spies" in the important households of the city, sometimes recruiting new agents by leaving a Voodoo poppet, in the dark of night, that was stuck with pins or a wax ball covered with feathers, at the door of a black servant who worked in a household that interested her. Usually the terrified victim would come to her begging to be "uncrossed." Marie would generously agree to help them in return for the servant supplying information about their superiors. Her spy system covered not only the leaders of society, but most of the city's political leaders and she had a thriving business in the sale of gris-gris, hexes, and protection. By the 1850s she was held in respect and fear by almost everyone in New Orleans, high or low, but through her good works via the Catholic Church and her volunteer nursing during epidemics and times of strife, she was loved by as many as feared her.

Her prowess as a Voodoo Priestess began to outshine those of Doctor John and although they remained friendly for the rest of his days, she took over the conducting of the St. John's Eve ceremonies. (Besides, Dr. John was being kept pretty busy with his 15 or so common law wives whom he had bought as slave girls!) Marie had learned a lot from Dr. John, and her natural flair for show business, plus a shrewd business sense had, by the 1850s, made her the most important woman in New Orleans. Voodoo was at its height, and her house on Rampart Street was at the very vortex of the movement.

In 1817, the New Orleans Council had forbidden blacks to gather for dancing or any other purpose, except on Sunday, and only in places approved by the mayor. Congo Square (now called Beauregard Square, a part of Armstrong Park) became the place where blacks met to dance and overtly worshipping their gods. Their white owners came to watch them do their "African foolishness." By 1830 there were several Voodoo Queens fighting for control of the Congo Square dances, as well as the secret ceremonies at Lake Ponchartrain. When "Mamzelle" Laveau decided that she would be queen, the others soon faded before her. Marie was aware of the sensation being caused by the secret rituals on the lake. She invited the public, the police, the press, and any thrill seekers to attend the forbidden fun. A fascinating part of her ceremonies was when she danced with her huge pet snake "Le Grand Zombi" who was reputedly the personification of the Voodoo Loa, "Damballah," while shaking a gourd rattle and chanting "Damballah, ye-ye-ye" to summon the god. She also began charging an admission fee for visitors, turning a profit for the movement. What was originally a black ritual soon was attracting about one-third white worshippers who were desirous of obtaining the "power" to regain a lost lover, to find a new lover, to eliminate a business partner or rival, or to destroy an enemy. On the side, Marie shrewdly organized parties for wealthy white men desirous of meeting beautiful black, mulatto, and quadroon mistresses. Soon Marie, with all the secret knowledge of New Orleans' boudoirs, her endless knowledge of spells, plus her flair for creating sensation, reigned supreme. Whites of every class sought her advice and help and blacks saw her as their leader. Judges would pay her as much as $1,000 for her help in winning elections, others would pay $10 for a love potion. It was very fashionable, though pricey, for society folk to have a Marie Laveau reading. She rarely charged blacks for her aid.

In 1869 Marie Laveau, at the age of 70, had her last performance as Voodoo Queen. She died in 1881 and, amazingly, the newspaper reports completely ignored her position as the Queen of Voodoo and painted her as a saintly figure who nursed the sick, prayed incessantly, and lived a pious life surrounded by her Catholic religion.

Her daughter Marie (II) was born in 1827 and in adulthood looked almost exactly like her mother. Somewhere along the line, to relieve the pressure of too many public appearances, she began appearing in ceremonies in her mother's place. As Marie (I) aged, the public would not see the frail and forgetful old lady her mother was becoming. Having inherited her mother's reputation she was able to control the press of the day via their fear of her putting a hex on them. Marie Laveau's fabled beauty seemed unbelievable and only bolstered her power. Although Marie II tried to continue in her mother's footsteps, she seemed to inspire more fear than compassion. She seemed to relax her Voodoo leadership, conducting fewer rituals and ceremonies, concentrating rather on holding lavish parties at the Maison Blanche for white men, politicians, and high officials, where she

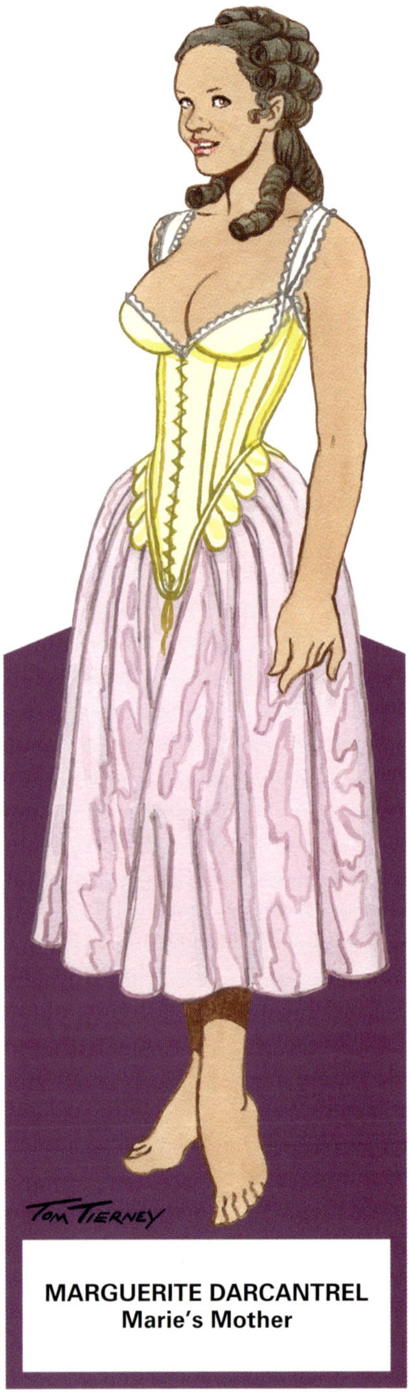

MARGUERITE DARCANTREL
Marie's Mother

A yellow satin boned corset, laced down the front with Piccadills at the waist, worn over a lavender watered taffeta petticoat. Powdered hair.

CHARLES LAVEAU
Marie's Father

A buttoned white cotton shirt with ruffled sleeve frills. Natural color knee length underpants are tied at the knees over yellow stockings.

Low-cut work dress with a striped bodice with rolled-up sleeves over a white chemise pulled forward forming an apron over a yellow underskirt.

Formal black hammer tail day coat over a green satin waistcoat worn with yellow court knee pants with white silk stockings. Black silk top hat, white cravat.

MARIE LAVEAU
Debutante & young matron

A lavender silk dinner dress with a low cut bodice and dropped sleeves. The V-bodice is attached to a full, gathered skirt.

A high-waisted, Empire styled visiting dress with polka dotted bodice and sleeves over a straight cut skirt. White straw jockey bonnet.

A low-cut Empire styled pale blue tunic topped party dress for summer with short puffed sleeves, worn over a daringly split dancing skirt.

A petal scalloped party gown in three shades of pink. The petticoats have been tucked up under the outer skirt to accommodate her Voodoo dance.

For marketing, a long sleeved plaid cotton dress with a full pleated skirt worn under a lightweight green shawl. Straw slippers and a turban (tignon).

A dressy yellow silk version of a work dress, trimmed in white flounces; a fitted bodice over a gathered skirt, which features a modified train.

JACQUES PARIS
Marie's first husband

For working he wears only an old pair of striped work pants.

CHRISTOPHE GLAMPION
Could he have been Jacques Paris in disguise?

Carpenters work clothes of blue broadcloth shirt with cotton work pants.

DOCTOR JOHN BAYOU
Voodoo priest and Marie's mentor.

Note his scarred and tattooed face and body

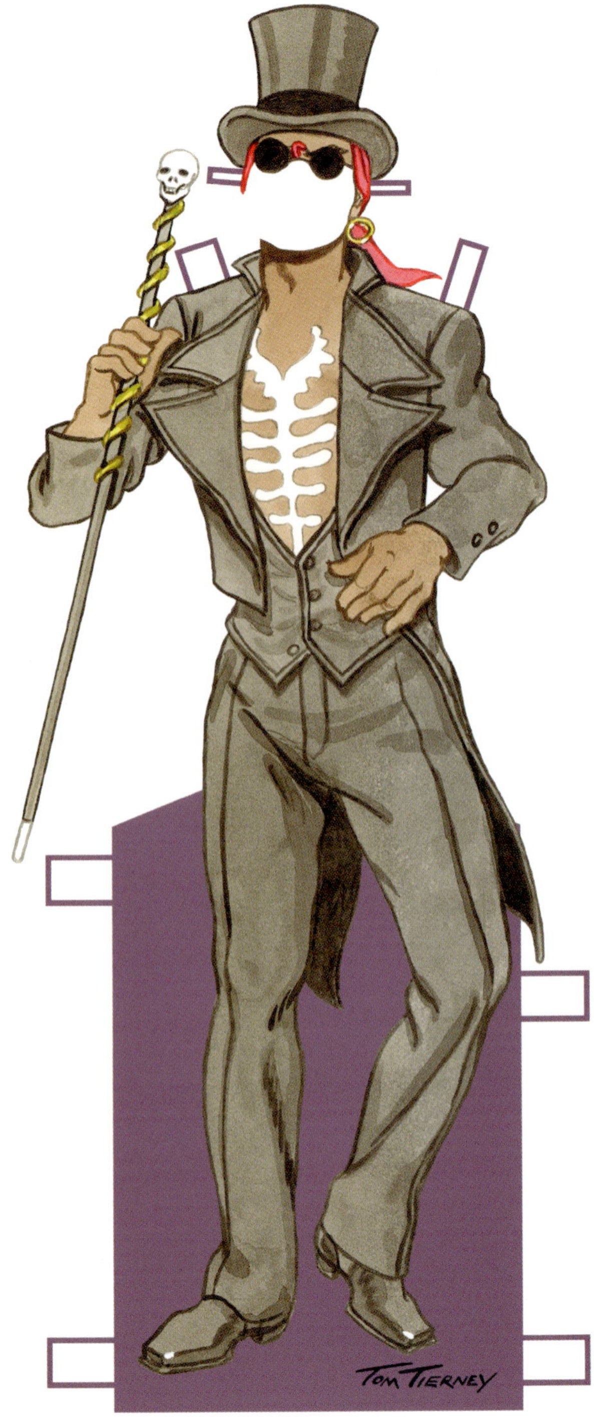

Dr. John is dressed like Baron Samedi, Loa, or god of the Cemetery (or death) in top hat, tailcoat, and walking cane.

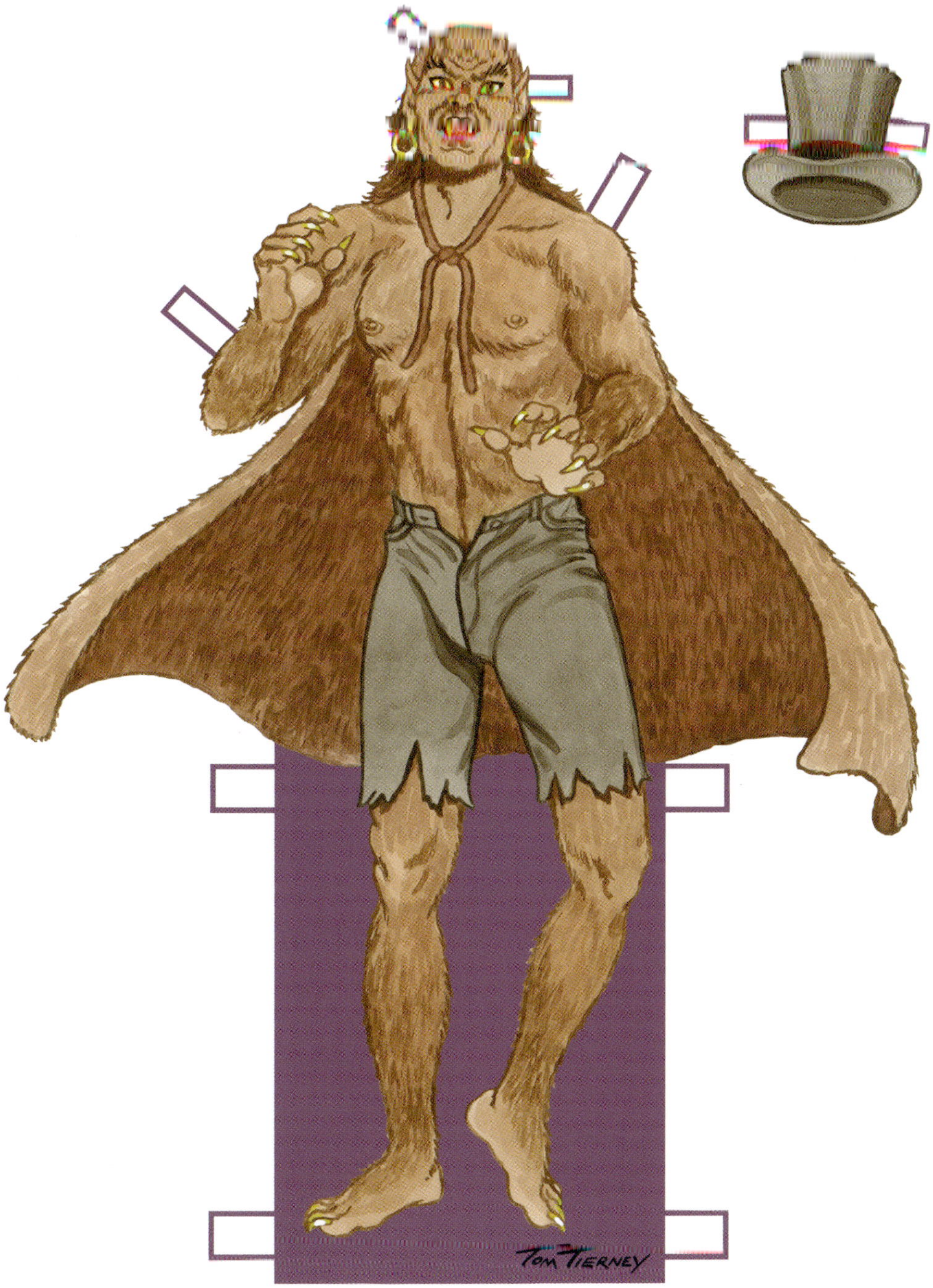

LOUP GAROU

Many Voodooists believed that Dr. John could become a "loup garou" or "werewolf."

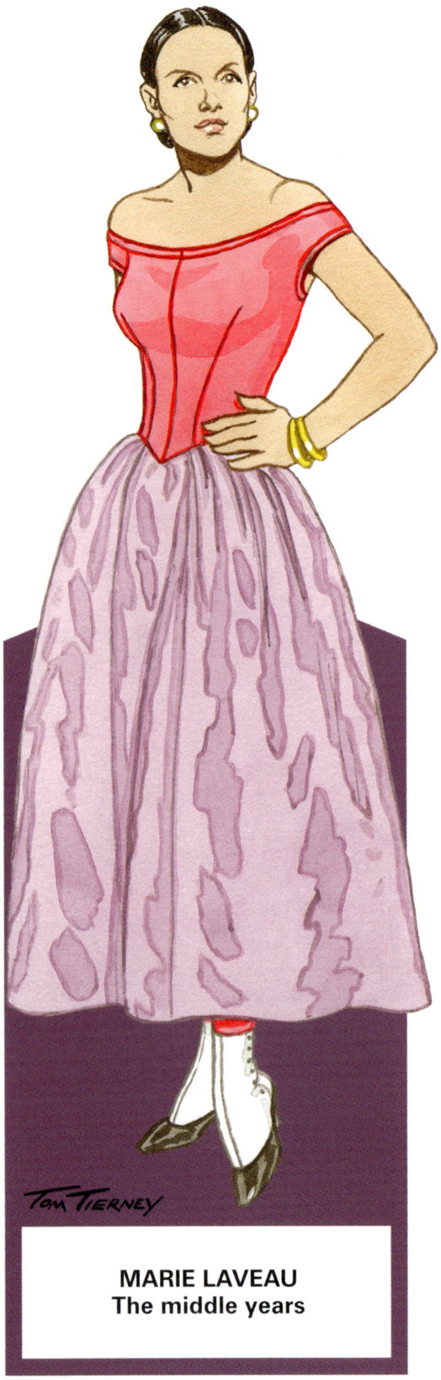

She wears a silk corselet with a taffeta petticoat.

Marie dressed as Erzulie, the beautiful Loa of feminine attractiveness.

As a hair-dresser in a sedate black work dress with mutton-chop puffed sleeves and a print shawl.

For her nursing duties, Marie chose a simple white cotton gown worn with a veil.

MARIE
Her later years

Wearing a blue cotton shift with a simple striped head cloth, Marie is prepared for simple chores at home.

Marie, with Zombi, dressed for a blood sacrifice in a polka dot blouse and hiked up skirts. Gold striped tignon

Ombre pink gown under a blue and gold Chinese shawl. The tignon, or turban, with seven tied points connotes Voodoo royalty.

Dancing with Zombi in a red and gold corset and skirt over a white under dress with huge caught-up sleeves.

Dancing with Zombi in a swirling, red, layered dress trimmed in white ruffles. At her waist she often wore a blue bird.

Although she probably never actually dressed this way, Marie is shown garbed like the "Pope of Voodoo."

A three-tiered green dirndl skirt worn under a royal blue stole. She holds a bag of gris-gris and wears a tignon.

From this point onward, these figures will be the dolls for the rest of the book. When dressed, they will represent some of the most popular loas or gods of Voodoo.

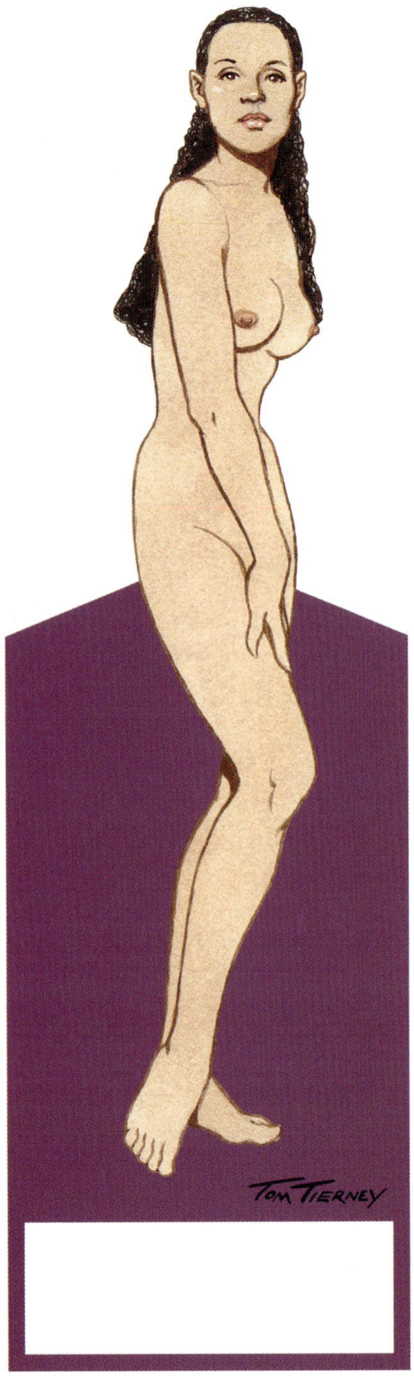

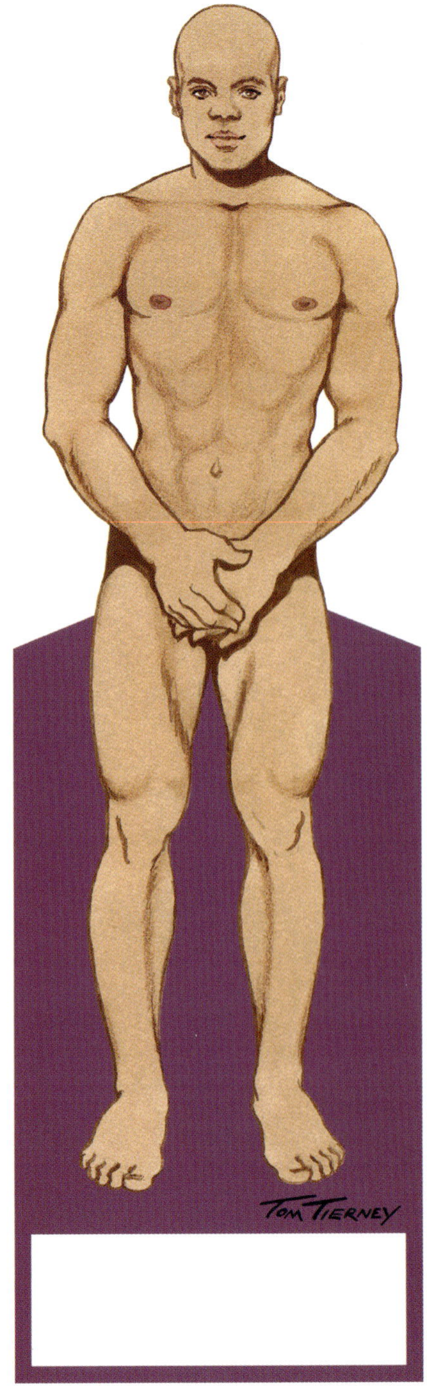

Left and Right are the MARASSA or divine twins, female and male, who represent the elemental forces of the universe. (They are often depicted as children) Before any voodoo meeting they must be acknowledged, but they cannot be summoned, as are other loas, in that their presence is always there. They are sometimes shown as triplets. In Voodoo the birth of twins is considered a special blessing, triplets even more so.

DAMBALLAH is the eldest and the chief of all the loas. He is a primordial serpent deity who created the world and the gods. He holds the earth in his coils and when he shifts about it causes earthquakes. Before any Voodoo ceremony can start he must be saluted. He is of such antiquity that he never speaks.

AYIDA WEDO is DAMBALLAH'S wife and is the great rainbow snake representing all aspects of fertility. For sacrifice both Ayida and Damballah favor eggs, pure water, and white chickens.

PAPA LEGBA is the gatekeeper of the spirit world, the remover of obstacles, and the creator of opportunities. All ceremonies must begin and end with saluting him and speaking through him to the other loas. He is most often seen as a kindly old man.

ERZULIE FREDDA is the most feminine aspect and represents love, beauty, and romance. She loves dancing, music, the arts, jewelry and pretty clothes, mirrors and combs. Her symbol is the heart and her colors are pink and white. The embodiment of femininity, she is also associated with *gay* men.

ERZULIE DANTOR is often depicted as dark skinned, sometimes scarred, and holding a babe protectively with a knife in her hand. She is a fierce protector of women and children. She is also the protector of lesbians.

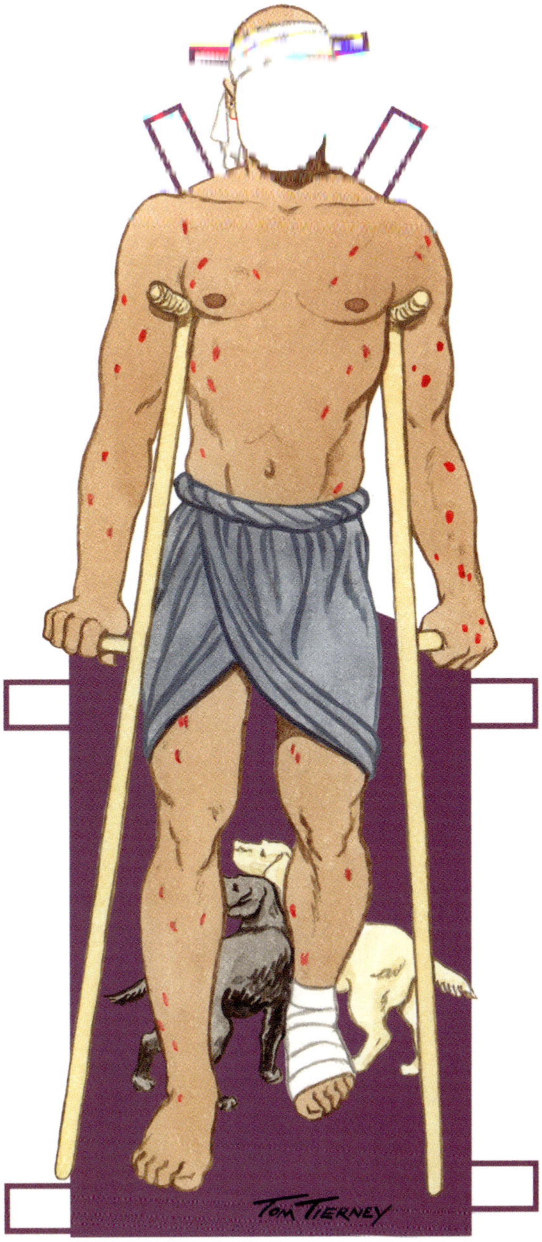

Babalu Aye is an Orisha or emissary of the Loas. He can both cause disease or heal it. His Christian symbol is St.. Lazarus. Many supplicants today appeal to him to ward off or cure AIDS. His symbols are crutches, body sores, and two dogs.

LA SIREN (sometimes called AMAYA) rules over the ocean and thence the world. She is another aspect of Erzulie. She is the wife of Agwe, the Loa of the Sea, and is the beautiful mermaid Loa of wealth and treasure. Very beautiful, rather vain, always restless, she rules the moon. (As AMAYA, she protects pregnant women, children, and gay men).

AGWE, the Loa of the Ocean, controls storms, ships, fishermen, sailors, and all aquatic life along with his wife, La Siren, over fishermen, sailors, fish and aquatic life. Offerings to him are placed on a small raft and floated on the sea or a river. He sometimes appears in a sailor's garb, though most often in an admiral's uniform.

BRIGITTE (sometimes called OYA) is the Loa of the marketplace (in New Orleans, the French Market). The marketplace is a metaphor for civilization, and she stands at the crossroads between value and the goods sold. In short, she can help one survive on little, or to use profits well.

ELEGUA, "the Trickster," is an aspect of Loco and Papa Legba. One must take care in one's requests of him!

OYA (an aspect of Maman Brigitte) is the Loa of change. She rules over the winds and hurricanes. Practitioners call on her when a great change is needed. She also guards the gates of cemeteries.

NAGO SHANGO is one of New Orleans most powerful Loas. He is the spirit of storms and fire. He carries an axe or a machete in one hand and lightning in the other. One of his favorite sacrifices is rum poured on the ground and then set afire. He can also protect against crime.

MAMAN BRIGITTE (Grande Brigitte) is the matron of the Guèdè family all of whom are associated with death.

BARON SAMEDI (Cimetière) is Maman Bridgitte's husband and the principal Loa of Death. Together they guard the cemetery and all graves that are marked with a cross. Both wear dark glasses, love cigarettes and dancing, drink rum saturated with peppers, and general carousing. Perhaps death is not as sad an adventure as we are led to fear!

was reputed to be able to fulfill any man's desires for a girl, for a price. Even so, her establishment was never raided by the police for fear that if they crossed Marie she might "hoodoo" them.

No one is absolutely sure where either Marie Laveau is buried and there are various sites that have been suggested. There is a vault in St. Louis Cemetery No 1 with the name Marie Philome Clapion (Marie II?) dated 1897. Marie I's obituary suggests that she too was buried in St. Louis Cemetery No. 1, in the Laveau-Glapion tomb, but no definitive marker for her bones still exists, although most commercial Voodoo tours tout it as her final resting place. However, she still may not be at rest, as both Maries have been reported to haunt New Orleans in various human and animal forms.

Note: This treatise is only a surface explanation, sometimes fictionalized, of Marie Laveau's life and times. Nor does it purport to fully describe all the Voodoo Loas or gods, its ceremonies, nor any of its spells. For deeper knowledge and clarity on this subject it is recommended that you consult an expert practitioner, such as a mambo or a hungan. There are also many books on the subject that can be found on the web as well as much generalized information to be gleaned from that same source.

Designed by "Sue"
Type set in Zurich BT

ISBN: 978-0-7643-3191-6
Printed in China

Schiffer Books are available at special discounts for bulk purchases for sales promotions or premiums. Special editions, including personalized covers, corporate imprints, and excerpts can be created in large quantities for special needs. For more information contact the publisher:

Published by Schiffer Publishing Ltd.
4880 Lower Valley Road
Atglen, PA 19310
Phone: (610) 593-1777; Fax: (610) 593-2002
E-mail: Info@schifferbooks.com

For the largest selection of fine reference books on this and related subjects, please visit our web site at:
www.schifferbooks.com
We are always looking for people to write books on new and related subjects. If you have an idea for a book please contact us at the above address.

This book may be purchased from the publisher.
Include $5.00 for shipping.
Please try your bookstore first.
You may write for a free catalog.

In Europe, Schiffer books are distributed by
Bushwood Books
6 Marksbury Ave.
Kew Gardens
Surrey TW9 4JF England
Phone: 44 (0) 20 8392-8585; Fax: 44 (0) 20 8392-9876
E-mail: info@bushwoodbooks.co.uk
Website: www.bushwoodbooks.co.uk
Free postage in the U.K., Europe; air mail at cost.